ABUSED AS DOGS IN YOUNG GENERATION

Flexible Properties Of The nerves In Brain Science And Human Relationship

By

Benjamin Micah

Table of content

Presentation

Section 1
Tina's reality

Section 2
To Your Benefit

PRESENTATION

It's difficult to Envision today, yet when I was in clinical school in the mid 1980s analysts didn't give a lot of consideration to the enduring harm that mental injury can deliver. Indeed, even less thought was given to how injury could hurt youngsters.

It wasn't viewed as important. Kids were accepted to be normally "strong," with a natural capacity. At the point when I turned into a youngster specialist and neuroscientist, it was not my objective to disprove this off track hypothesis. However at that point, as a youthful specialist, I started to see in the lab that upsetting encounters, especially in early life, could change the cerebrums of youthful creatures.

Various studies demonstrated that even minor pressure during earliest stages could have a super durable effect on the design and the science of the mind and, subsequently, on conduct. I thought: for what reason couldn't similar be valid for people?

That question turned out to be considerably more remarkable to me as I started my clinical work with upset kids. I before long tracked down that by far most of my patients had lives loaded up with disarray, disregard, as well as viciousness. Obviously, these youngsters weren't "quickly returning" any other way they could not have possibly been taken to a youth psychiatry facility! They'd endured injury , for example, being assaulted or seeing homicide that would have had most therapists taking into account the conclusion of post-awful pressure issue (PTSD), had they have been grown-ups with mental issues. But these kids were being treated like their accounts of injury were superfluous, and they'd "incidentally" created side effects, like wretchedness or consideration issues that frequently required medicine.

Obviously, the conclusion of PTSD was just brought into psychiatry in 1980, From the outset, it was viewed as something interesting, a condition that just impacted a minority of troopers who had been crushed by battle encounters. Yet, soon similar sorts of side effects meddling contemplations about the horrendous mishap, flashbacks, disturbed rest, a feeling of illusion, an elevated alarm reaction, outrageous uneasiness started to be depicted in assault survivors, casualties of cataclysmic events, and individuals who'd had or seen dangerous mishaps or wounds. Presently the condition is accepted to influence something like 7% of all Americans and a great many people are aware about the thought that injury can make significant and enduring impacts. From the repulsions of the 9/11 psychological militant assaults to the consequence of Tropical storm Katrina, we perceive that disastrous occasions can make permanent imprints on the brain. We now know from my examination and that of so many others has at last shown that the effect is far more noteworthy on youngsters than it is on grown-ups.

I have made it my all consuming purpose to comprehend what injury means for kids
furthermore, to foster creative ways of assisting them with adapting to it. I have treated and
concentrated on kids confronted with probably the absolute most awful encounters possible from the enduring survivors of the Branch Davidian religion
blaze in Waco, Texas, to disregarded Eastern European vagrants, to slaughter survivors.

I have additionally assisted courts with figuring out the destruction of misinformed "Sinister Ceremony Misuse" arraignments in light of constrained allegations from tormented, panicked youngsters.
I have given a valiant effort to help kids who saw their folks' killings, and those who've spent years tied in confines or secured in storage rooms.
While most youngsters endure nothing as dreadful as what a significant number of my patients have gone through, the intriguing youngster gets away from injury completely. By moderate assessments, around 40% of American kids will have somewhere around one possibly damaging experience by age eighteen: this incorporates the demise of a parent or kin, continuous actual maltreatment, or potentially disregard, sexual maltreatment, or the experience of a serious mishap, regular fiasco aggressive behaviour at home or other rough violations.

In 2004 alone an expected 3,000,000 authority reports of youngster misuse or disregard was made to government youngster assurance offices; around 872,000 of these cases were affirmed. Obviously, the genuine number of manhandled and dismissed kids is far higher in light of the fact that most cases are never detailed and a few veritable cases can't be adequately certified for official move to be made. In one enormous review, around one of every eight kids younger than seventeen revealed some type of serious abuse by grown-ups inside the previous year, and around 27% of ladies and 16 percent men report as grown-ups having been physically deceived during adolescence.

In a public overview conducted in 1995, 6 percent of moms and 3 percent fathers even conceded to genuinely manhandling

their youngsters no less than once. Moreover, up to ten million American kids are subjected to abusive behaviour at home every year and 4 percent of American kids younger than fifteen lose a parent to death every year. Likewise, every year nearly 800,000 kids will invest energy in child care and millions more are
casualties of cataclysmic events and pulverising car crashes.

In spite of the fact that I don't intend to suggest that these kids will be harshly "harmed" by these encounters, the most safe assessments propose that at some random time, in excess of 8,000,000 American kids experience the ill effects of serious, diagnosable, injury related mental issues.
Millions more experience less serious yet upsetting outcomes. About 33% of youngsters who are manhandled will have some reasonable
mental issues therefore and research keeps on showing how indeed, even apparently absolutely "physical" issues like coronary illness, weight, and
Malignant growth can be bound to influence damaged youngsters later in their lives.
Grown-ups' reactions to youngsters during and after horrendous mishaps can make a gigantic distinction in these possible results both for good and for sick. Throughout the long term research from my lab and numerous others has created a
a much more extravagant comprehension of how injury treats youngsters and how we can assist them with mending from it.

In 1996 I established The ChildTrauma Foundation, an interdisciplinary gathering of experts committed to working on the existences of
high-risk youngsters and their families. We proceed with our clinical work nevertheless have a lot to learn, yet our essential objective is to bring medicines in light of the best of our current

information to other people. We train individuals who work with kids whether they are guardians or investigators, cops or judges, social labourers, doctors, policymakers, or legislators to comprehend the best approaches to limiting the effect of injury and augmenting recuperation. We talk with government organisations and different gatherings to help then execute the prescribed procedures in managing these issues.

My partners and I travel widely all over the planet, addressing guardians, specialists, teachers, youngster security labourers, and policing,
as well as significant level partners like authoritative bodies or boards furthermore, concerned corporate pioneers. This book is important for our endeavours.

In Abused as dogs the young generation , you'll meet a portion of the youngsters who showed me the main examples about what injury means for youthful individuals. Also, you'll gain what they need from us, their folks and gatekeepers, their PCPs, their administration assuming that they are to construct sound lives. You'll perceive the way awful experience marks youngsters, how it influences their characters, and their ability for physical and profound development.
You'll meet my most memorable patient, Tina, whose experience of misuse brought back
to me the effect of injury on kids' minds. You'll meet a fearless little young lady named Sandy, who at three years old must be placed in an observer
insurance program, and who showed me the significance of permitting a kid to control parts of her treatment. You'll meet an astounding kid called
Justin, who showed me how youngsters can recuperate from unspeakable hardship. Every youngster I've worked with the Branch Davidian kids, who breathed easy in light of really focusing on one another; Laura, whose body didn't develop

until she had a real sense of security and cherished; Peter, a Russian vagrant whose 1st grade cohorts turned into his "specialists" assisted my partners and me with setting a new piece in the riddle, permitting us to propel our treatment for damaged youngsters and their families.

Our work brings us into people groups' lives when they are generally frantic, alone, miserable, apprehensive, and injured, however generally the narratives you'll peruse. Here are examples of overcoming adversity: accounts of trust, endurance, and win. Shockingly, it is frequently while meandering through the close to home bloodletting left by the most obviously awful of humanity that we track down the best of mankind also.

At last, what decides how youngsters endure injury, genuinely, inwardly, or mentally, is whether individuals around them, especially the grown-ups, ought to have the option to trust and depend upon them with adoration, backing, and consolation. Fire can warm or consume, water can extinguish or suffocate, and wind can touch or cut. Thus it is with human connections: we can both make and annihilate, sustain and threaten, damage and recuperate one another.

In this book, you will learn about exceptional kids whose accounts can assist us with better figuring out the nature and force of human connections.
Albeit a large number of these young men and young ladies have had encounters undeniably more
As outrageous as most families will experience (and thank heavens for that), their accounts convey examples for all guardians that can assist their kids with adapting with the inescapable burdens and kinds of life.

Working with damaged and abused kids has additionally made me consider cautiously about the idea of humanity and the distinction between
mankind and humankind. Not all people are accommodating. A person has to figure out how to become empathetic. That interaction and how it can some of the time turn out badly is one more part of what's going on with this book.

The tales here investigate the circumstances essential for the advancement of compassion and
those that are logical, all things being equal, to deliver savagery and indifference.
They uncover how youngsters' cerebrums develop and are shaped by individuals around them. They likewise uncover how obliviousness, neediness, viciousness, sexual maltreatment, mayhem, and disregard can unleash ruin after developing minds and incipient characters.

I have for quite some time been keen on grasping human turn of events, and particularly in attempting to sort out why certain individuals grow up to be useful, capable, and kind individuals, while others answer maltreatment by incurring a greater amount of it for other people. My work has uncovered to me an incredible manage moral turn of events, the foundations of fiendishness, and how hereditary propensities and ecological impacts can shape basic choices, which thus influence later decisions and, eventually, who we end up being. I don't really trust in "the maltreatment excuse" for brutal or destructive way of behaving, yet I have
observed that there are complicated connections starting in youth that influence our capacity to imagine decisions and that may later restrict our capacity to pursue the most ideal choices. My work has taken me to the crossing point of psyche and mind, to the spot where we simply decide and encounter impacts that decide if

or then again not we become sympathetic and really human. The Abused as Dogs the young Generation, offers some of what I've realised there. Notwithstanding their agony and dread,
The kids in this book and numerous others like them have shown perfect boldness and mankind, and they give me trust. From them, I have learned
much about misfortune, love, and recuperating.
The centre illustrations these kids have shown me are applicable to all of us.
Since to comprehend injury we really want to grasp memory.

In request to see the value in how kids mend we really want to comprehend how they learn
to adore, how they adapt to difficulties, and what stress means for them. What's more, by
perceiving the horrendous effect that viciousness and danger can have on the
ability to cherish and work, we can come to all the more likely figure out ourselves and
to sustain individuals in our lives, particularly the kids.

Section 1

Tina's reality

Tina was my most memorable kid patient, only seven years of age when I met her. She sat in the sitting area of the College of Chicago Youngster Psychiatry Center, little and delicate, crouched with her mom and kin, uncertain what to anticipate from her new specialist.

As I drove her to my office and shut the entryway, it was difficult to tell which one of us was more anxious: the three-foot-tall African-American young lady with carefully perfect interlaces or the six-foot-two white person with a long mane of uncontrollable twists.

Tina sat on my lounge chair for a minute, looking at me, up and down. Then, she strolled across the room, crept into my lap, and cuddled in.

I was contacted. Golly, what something pleasant to do. What a sweet kid. She moved her hand to my groyne and attempted to open my zipper. I was as of now not restless. Presently, I was miserable. I grasped her hand, moved it from my thighs, and painstakingly took her off my lap.

The morning before I initially met with Tina I read through her "outline" — one little piece of paper with negligible data taken during a telephone interview with our admission specialist. Tina lived with her mom, Sara, and two more youthful kin. Sara had called the youngster psychiatry centre since the little girl's school had demanded that she get her assessed.

Tina had been "forceful and improper" with her colleagues. She'd uncovered herself, gone after different youngsters, utilised sexual language, and attempted to get them to take part in sex play. She didn't focus in class and frequently declined to follow her bearings. The most pertinent history the diagram contained was that Tina had been manhandled for a two-year time frame that began when she was four and finished at the point when she was six.

The culprit was a sixteen-year-old kid, her sister's child. He had attacked both Tina and her youthful sibling, Michael, while their mom was working. Tina's mother was single. Poor, yet presently not on open help, at the time Sara worked the lowest pay permitted by law to work at an odds-and-ends shop to help her loved ones. The main childcare she could bear was a casual course of action with her nearby neighbour.

That neighbour, sadly, frequently left the youngsters with her child so she could get things done. What's more, her child was wiped out. He tied the youngsters up and assaulted them, sodomised them with unfamiliar articles, and took steps to kill them if they told me. At last, his mom got him and ended the maltreatment.

Sara at absolutely no point ever allowed her neighbour to focus on her youngsters in the future, yet the harm had been finished. (The kid was arraigned; he went to treatment, not prison.) Here we were, after one year. The little girl had difficult issues, the mother had no assets, and I didn't understand anything about mishandled youngsters.

"Here. How about we go variety," I expressed delicately as I took her from my lap. She appeared to be vexed. Has she disappointed me? Could I blow up? She restlessly concentrated all over with her dull-coloured eyes, watching my developments, paying attention to my voice for a few nonverbal prompts to assist her with detecting this association.

My behaviour didn't fit with her inward inventory of past encounters with men. She had just referred to men as sexual stalkers: no cherishing father, no steady granddad, no thoughtful uncle or defensive, more established siblings had contacted her. The main grown-up guys she'd met were her mother's many times unseemly because of her victimizer.

Experience had instructed her that men needed sex, either from her or her mom. So very coherently according to her point of view, she accepted that is what I needed also.

How would it be a good idea for me to respond? How would you change ways of behaving or convictions, got into place from long periods of involvement, with one hour of treatment seven days?

None of My experience and preparation had set me up for this young lady. I didn't grasp her. Did she cooperate with everybody like they needed sex from her, even ladies and young ladies? Was this the main way she knew how to make companions? Was her forceful and incautious way of behaving at school related to this? Did she suppose I was dismissing her and how should that influence her?

It was 1987. I was an individual in Kid and Juvenile Psychiatry at the College of Chicago, simply beginning the last two years of the absolute best clinical preparation in the country. I'd had very nearly twelve years of Postgraduate preparation.

I was a MD, and a PhD and had completed three years as a clinical and general psychiatry occupant. I ran a fundamental neuroscience research lab that concentrated on the pressure reaction frameworks in the cerebrum. I had realised about synapses and mind frameworks and their intricate organisations

Also, science. I had gone through years attempting to figure out the human psyche. Furthermore, after everything that could be remembered to do was this:

I plunked down with Tina at a little table set up in my office and I gave her a bunch of pastels and a shading book. She opened it up and paged through. "Might I at any point be interested in this?" she asked delicately, obviously uncertain what to do in these abnormal circumstances. "Sure," I told her.

"Would it be advisable for me to make her dress blue or red?" I asked Tina. "Red." "Alright." She held up her hued page for my endorsement, "Exceptionally decent." I said. She grinned. For the following forty minutes, we sat on the floor, next to each other, shading discreetly, coming over to acquire pastels, showing our advancement to one another, and attempting to become accustomed to being in a similar space with an outsider.

At the point when the meeting was finished, I strolled Tina back to the centre holding up the region. Her mom was holding a youthful baby and conversing with her four-year-old child. Sara expressed gratitude toward me and we set up one more arrangement for the following week.

As they left I realised I expected to converse with a boss with more experience who could assist me with sorting out some way to help this young lady. Oversight in psychological wellness preparation is a deceptive term. At the point when I was a clinical understudy figuring out how to place in a focal line, run a code, or draw blood, there were more established, more experienced doctors present to train, reprove, help, and instruct me.

I frequently got prompt generally negative input. While it was the case that we followed the model "watch one, do one, show one," a more senior, experienced clinician was in every case nearby to assist during any communications with patients. Not so for psychiatry.

As a learner, when I was with a patient, or a patient Furthermore, her family, I was quite often working alone. After meeting with the patient once in a while numerous times I examined the case with my manager. While preparing a kid psychiatrist, individuals will regularly have a few managers for clinical work.

Frequently I would introduce a similar kid or on the other hand issue to numerous managers to accumulate their various impressions and acquire from their numerous, ideally correlative, bits of knowledge. It is an intriguing interaction that has a few noteworthy qualities yet in addition has some clear lacks, which I was going to find.

I put forth Tina's perspective to my most memorable manager, Dr. Robert Stine. He was youthful, serious, scholarly, and in preparing to turn into a psychoanalyst. He kept a full facial hair growth and wore seemingly a similar outfit consistently: a dark suit, a dark tie, and a white shirt. He appeared to be a ton more intelligent than me.

He utilised mental language easily: "the maternal introject," "object relations," "counter-transaction," and "oral obsession." And at the point when he did, I'd look at him without flinching and attempt to properly look serious and smart, gesturing as though what he was talking about was clearing things up for me: "Ah, yes. Alright. All things considered, that's what I'll remember."

However, I was thinking, "What on earth would he say he is discussing?" I gave a short yet formal show, portraying Tina's side effects, history, family, and grievances from her school, as well as itemising the key components of my most memorable encounter with her. Dr. Stine took notes. At the point when I did not know. I slowed down. Clinical preparation shows a youthful doctor to act considerably less obvious than the person is.

Also, I was uninformed. Dr. Stine detected this and recommended we utilise the analytic aid for mental problems, the Symptomatic and Measurable Manual (DSM). By then, it was the DSM III. Like clockwork or so it is updated to remember refreshes for research and groundbreaking thoughts regarding messes. This interaction is directed by true standards yet is entirely vulnerable to sociopolitical and other nonscientific processes. For instance, homosexuality was once considered a "jumble" in the DSM and presently it isn't.

In any case, the fundamental issue with the DSM right up until now is that it is an inventory of problems in light of records of side effects. It is similar to a PC manual composed of a board without any information on the machine's real equipment or programming, a manual that endeavours to decide the reason for and solution for the PC's issues by requesting that you consider the sounds it makes.

As I probably was aware from my exploration and preparation, the frameworks in that "machine" for this situation, the human cerebrum are extremely mind-boggling.

Thus, I couldn't help thinking that the same "yield" may be caused by quite a few unique issues inside it. Yet, the DSM doesn't represent this. "So she is negligent, has a discipline issue, imprudent, rebellious, resistant, oppositional, and generally disapproves of her companions. She meets symptomatic models for lack of ability to concentrate consistently on Confusion and oppositional resistant turmoil," Dr. Stine provoked.

Better believe it, I surmise so." I said. However, it didn't feel right to me. Tina was encountering something else or something else than what was depicted by those analytic names. I knew from my examination of the mind that the frameworks associated with controlling and concentrating were particularly complicated.

I likewise knew that numerous natural and hereditary variables could impact them. Wasn't naming Tina "resistant" deceiving, considering that her "rebelliousness" was possibly a consequence of her exploitation? Shouldn't something be said about the disarray that made her think that sexual ?.

Is conducting with grown-ups and peers openly ordinary? Shouldn't something be said about her discourse Also, language delays? Also, assuming she could not concentrate consistently, could the sexual maltreatment be significant in understanding how to treat it? Does somebody like her?

However, I didn't bring up these issues. I just checked out. Dr Stine and gestured as though I was engrossing what he was instructing me. "Go set out to find out about psychopharmacology for ADD. We can discuss this one week from now," he prompted.

I left Dr. Stine feeling befuddled and frustrated. This being a kid therapist? I had been prepared as a general (grown-up) specialist and knew about the impediments of oversight, and the limits of our analytic methodology, yet I was not the slightest bit acquainted with the unavoidable issues of the youngsters I was seeing.

They were socially minimised, formatively deferred, significantly harmed, and shipped off our facility so we could "fix" things that to me didn't appear to be fixable with the apparatuses we had available to us. How should a couple of hours a month and a remedy change Tina's viewpoint and conduct? Did Dr. Stine accept that Ritalin or some other ADD medication would settle this young lady's issues?

Luckily, I had one more boss too: a shrewd and great man, a genuine monster in the field of psychiatry, Dr. Jarl Dyrud. Like me, he was from North Dakota, and we hit it off right away. Like Dr. Stine, Dr. Dyrud was prepared with a logical strategy. However, he additionally had long stretches of genuine experience attempting to comprehend and help individuals. He had let that experience, not simply Freud's speculations, formed his point of view.

He listened cautiously as I portrayed Tina. At the point when I was done, he grinned at me and said, "Did you appreciate shading with her?" I thought briefly and said, "No doubt. Indeed I did."

Dr. Dyrud said, "Extremely pleasant beginning. So let me know more." I began to list Tina's

side effects and the grumblings the grown-ups had about her ways of behaving. "No, no. Inform me concerning her. Not about her side effects." "Your meaning could be a little more obvious." "Where does she reside? What is her condo-like, when does she go to rest, and what does she do during the day? Inform me concerning her."

I conceded that I didn't have a clue about any of that data. "Invest some energy getting to know her, not her side effects. Learn about her life," he exhorted. For the following couple of meetings, Tina and I invested energy in shading or playing straightforward games and discussing what she got a kick out of the chance to do. At the point when I ask kids like Tina what they need to be at the point at which they grow up, they frequently answer with "Assuming I grow up," because they've seen such a lot of genuine demise and viciousness at home and in their areas that arriving at adulthood appears to be unsure.

In our discussions at times, Tina would let me know that she needed to be an educator, and at different times she said she needed to be a stylist, all with the completely customary, quickly changing cravings of a young lady of her age.

In any case, as we examined particulars of these different objectives, it required some investment before I was ready to assist her with perceiving that the future can be something you plan for, something you can foresee and try and change, as opposed to a progression of unanticipated occasions that simply happen to you.

I likewise conversed with her mom about her conduct in school and at home and figured out more about her life. There was, obviously, the everyday daily schedule of school. After school, tragically, there was much of the time a few hours between the time Tina and her more youthful sibling returned home and the time Sara got off from work. Sara had her kids call her to check in, and there were neighbours close by they could contact in a crisis, yet she would rather not risk more guardian misuse.

So the kids remained at home alone, normally sitting in front of the television. Also, in some cases, Sara conceded, as a result of what they'd both experienced, there was sexualized play.

Sara was a long way from a careless mother, yet attempting to take care of three youthful youngsters frequently left her depleted, overpowered, and debilitated. Any parent would have been unable to adapt to the feelings of these damaged youngsters. The family had a brief period to play or simply be together.

As in many monetarily lashed homes, there was in every case some squeezing need, a financial clinical, or close-to-home crisis that expected quick thoughtfulness regarding staying away from the fiasco, for example, vagrancy employment cutback, or overpowering obligation.

As my work with Tina proceeded with Sara generally grinning when she first saw me. The hour that Tina had treatment was one opportunity in her week when she didn't need to do anything to accompany her different youngsters.

Tina would get down to my office while I paused for a minute to goof with her younger sibling (he was getting help too yet with another person at an alternate time) andgrin at the child. At the point when I was certain they had gotten comfortable with something to possess them in the holding-up region, I'd rejoin Tina, who might be sitting at her little seat sitting tight for me.

"What would it be advisable for us to do today?" she would ask, checking the games out, shading books, and toys she had pulled from my racks and placed on the table. I would profess to consider every option while she'd take a gander at me with expectation.

My eyes would fix on a game on the table and say, "Mmm. What about we should play Activity?" She would chuckle, "Yes!" She directed our play. I gradually presented new ideas, such as pausing and suspecting, previously choosing what to do straight away.

Once in a while, she would immediately share some reality or some expectation or some trepidation with me. I would pose inquiries to get some lucidity. Then she would divert the connection back to play.

Also, Step by step, little by little, I got to know Tina. Later that fall, notwithstanding, Tina was late to treatment for a considerable length of time in a line. Since arrangements were just 60 minutes, this occasionally implied we would just have twenty minutes for our meetings. I committed the error of referencing this to Dr. Stine during a report looking into the issue. He raised his eyebrows and gazed at me. He appeared to be frustrated.

"What do you believe is happening here?" "I don't know. I think the mother appears to be pretty wrecked. You should decipher the obstruction." "Ok. Alright." What on God's green earth would he say he is discussing? Is he recommending that Tina doesn't have any desire to come to treatment and is some way or another driving her mom to be late? "You mean Tina's obstruction or the mother's?" I inquired.

"The mother left these kids at risk. She might be angry that This youngster is certainly standing out. She might believe that she should stay harmed,"he said.

"Gracious," I answered, not certain what to think. I knew that examiners frequently deciphered delay to treatment as an indication of "opposition" to change, yet that was starting to appear to be silly, particularly for this situation. The thought left no room for certifiable luck and appeared to make a special effort to fault individuals like Tina's mother, who, as should have been obvious, did all that could be within reach to get help for Tina.

It was hard for her to get to the facility. To get to the clinical focus, she needed to take three unique transports, which frequently arrived later than expected during the merciless Chicago winter; she had no childcare so she needed to bring every one of her youngsters; once in a while, she needed to get cash for the transport charge.

It appeared to me she was doing all that could be expected in a very troublesome circumstance. Presently, as I left the structure one frozen night, I saw Tina and her family were hanging tight for the transport home. They were remaining in obscurity and snow was gradually falling through the faint light of a nearby streetlamp.

Sara was holding the child and Tina was perched on the seat close to her sibling under the intense light of the bus station. The two kin sat near one another, clasping hands and gradually shaking their legs this way and that. Their feet didn't arrive at the ground and they kept time with one another, in a state of harmony. It was 6:45. Frosty virus. They wouldn't be home for one more hour at any rate.

I pulled my vehicle over, hidden, and watched them, trusting the transport would come rapidly. I felt regretful watching them from my warm vehicle. I figured I ought to give them a ride. Be that as it may, the field of psychiatry is extremely mindful of limits.

There should be unbreachable walls between patient and specialist, severe fringes that characterise the relationship in experiences that frequently In any case, such construction is needed. The standard typically sounded good to me, yet entirely like numerous restorative ideas that had been created in work with psychotic working-class grown-ups, it didn't appear to fit here.

At last, the transport came. I felt quite a bit better. The following week, I held up quite a while after our meeting before going to my vehicle. I attempted to let myself know that I was doing desk work, however, I didn't need to see the family remaining in the cold once more.

I was unable to quit pondering what could be off with the basic compassionate demonstration of giving somebody a ride home when it was cold out. Might it at some point slow down the remedial process? I went this way and that, however my heart continued to descend as an afterthought of graciousness.

A genuine, kind demonstration, it appeared to me, could have a more remedial effect than any counterfeit, sincerely controlled position that so frequently portrays "treatment."

It was a full winter in Chicago now and sharply, harshly cold. I eventually That's what let me know whether I saw the family once more, I'd give them a ride. It was the right thing to do. Also, one night in December as I went home and drove by the bus station, they were right there. I offered them a ride. Sara declined from the start,

saying she needed to stop at the supermarket on her way. In for a penny in for a pound, I thought. I proposed to drive them to the store. After some more wavering, she concurred and they generally climbed into my Toyota Corolla.

Miles from the clinical focus, Sara highlighted a corner store and I halted there. Holding her resting child, she checked out at me, uncertain whether to bring every one of the youngsters into the store with her.

"Here. I'll hold the child. We'll stand by here," I said conclusively. She was in the store for around ten minutes. We paid attention to the radio. Tina chimed in with the music. I was simply asking if the child wouldn't awaken. I gradually shook her, mirroring the mood that Tina's mom had utilised.

Sara emerged from the store with two weighty sacks. "Take these back there and contact nothing," she told Tina, putting the sacks on the secondary lounge. At the point when we showed up at her structure, I looked as Sara attempted to get out of the vehicle and stroll through the unshoveled snow on the walkway, shuffling the child, her handbag, and a sack of food.

Tina attempted to convey the other sack of food, however, it was excessively weighty for herself and she sneaked through the snow. I opened my entryway and got out, taking one pack from Tina and the other one from Sara.

"No. We can make due," she dissented. "I realise you can. In any case, this evening I can help." She checked out at me, not certain how to manage this. I detected her attempting to comprehend on the off chance that this was consideration or something evil. She appeared to be humiliated. I felt humiliated.

However, it still appeared ok to help. We as a whole strolled up three stairwells to their condo. Tina's mom got out her keys and opened three locks all without upsetting her resting child. How troublesome this mother's life was, I thought, in isolation, focusing on three kids, no cash, just roundabout and frequently dreary work, and a negative, more distant family close by. I remained at the limit of the entryway with the sacks in my arms, not having any desire to barge in.

"You can just put those on the table," Sara said as she strolled to the back of the one-room condo to put the child down on a sleeping pad against the wall. In two stages I was at the kitchen table. I put the packs down and looked around the room. There was one loveseat confronting a variety of TVs and a little end table with a couple of cups and grimy dishes on it.

On a little table with three unequalled seats close to the kitchenette, there was a portion of Wonder bread and a container of peanut butter. One twofold sleeping pad sat on the floor, with covers and cushions perfectly collapsed toward one side. Garments and papers were spread around.

An image of Martin Luther Ruler Jr. held tight to the wall, and close to it on either side were splendidly hued school representations of Tina and her siblings. On another wall balanced an image of Sara and the child, somewhat warped. The loft was warm.

Sara stood and clumsily said, "Thanks again for the ride." and I guaranteed her it had been no difficulty. The second was truly awkward. As I left and said, "See you all one week from now," Tina waved.

She and her little child sibling were taking care of some food. They were preferred acts over numerous youngsters I'd found in much better conditions; it appeared to me that they must be.

The commute home took me through the absolute least fortunate areas in Chicago. I felt remorseful. Blameworthy about the karma, the open doors, the assets, and the gifts I had been given, liable pretty much every one of the times I had griped about working excessively, or not getting credit for something I had done. I additionally felt I discovered significantly more about Tina.

She had experienced childhood in another way that was really affecting her badly. The world is so altogether different from mine. What's more, in some way or another that must be connected with the issues that carried her to see me. I didn't know precisely everything it was, yet, I realised there was a significant thing about how the world she grew up what's more, lived in had moulded her profound conduct, and social, and physical well-being.

Later I was reluctant to let anybody know what I'd done, that I'd driven a patient and her family home. More awful yet, I had halted at the store on the way and acquired a few basic foods. In any case, part of me couldn't have cared less. I realised I'd made the best decision. You simply don't let a youthful mother with two small kids and a child stand in a virus-like state.

I held up for about fourteen days and afterward, when I next met with Dr. Dyrud, I told him. "I saw them sitting tight for a means of transport and it was cold. So, I gave them a ride home,"

I said anxiously, examining his face for his response, very much like Tina had done with me. He chuckled as I gradually enlightened him concerning the degree of my offence.

At the point when I'd got done, he applauded together, saying, "Fantastic! We ought to do a home encounter with our patients as a whole." He grinned and sat back. "Fill me in regarding it." I was stunned. In a moment Dr. Dyrud's grin and the pleasure all over let me out of about fourteen days of annoying responsibility.

At the point when he asked what I'd learned I let him know that one second in that little condo had let me know more about the difficulties confronting Tina and her family than I might at any point have gained from any on-location meeting or interview.

Later in that first year of my youngster psychiatry cooperation Sara and her family moved to a loft nearer to the clinical focus, one twenty-minute transport ride away. The delay stopped. That's it "opposition " We kept on gathering one time per week.

Dr. Dyrus's Shrewdness and mentorship kept on being freeing for me. Like different instructors, clinicians, and scientists who had roused me, he supported investigation, interest, and reflection, at the same time, above all, gave me the fortitude to challenge existing convictions. Taking pieces and pieces from every one of my coaches, I started to foster a restorative methodology that looked to make sense of profound and social issues as side effects of brokenness inside the cerebrum.

In 1987 youngster psychiatry had not yet embraced neurosciences. The huge extension of exploration on the endless mental health that started during the 1980s and detonated during the 1990s ("the 10 years of the mind") had at this point to happen, not to mention impact clinical practice.

All things considered, there was dynamic resistance by numerous therapists and specialists to take an organic point of view on the human way of behaving.

Such a methodology was considered unthinking and dehumanising, like decreasing the way of behaving to natural corresponds consequently implying that everything was brought about by qualities, ruling out unrestrained choice and innovativeness, and no real way to consider natural variables like neediness. Transformative thoughts were viewed as even

more terrible, as in reverse bigot and misogynist hypotheses that justified the status quo and diminished human activity to creature drives. Since I was simply beginning in kid psychiatry, I didn't yet trust my own ability to think autonomously, to process and decipher precisely how the situation was playing out.

How should my contemplations about this be correct when none of the other laid-out specialists, the stars, and my guides were discussing or on the other hand, showing these things?

Luckily, Dr. Dyrud and a few of my different guides energised my propensity to incorporate neuroscience into my clinical contemplating Tina and different patients. What was happening in Tina's cerebrum? What was different about her cerebrum that made her more incautious and oblivious than different young ladies her age?

What had occurred in her quickly-creating mind when she had experienced these strange, sexualized encounters as a little child? Did the pressure of neediness influence her? Furthermore, for what reason did she have discourse and language delays?

Dr. Dyrud used to highlight his head as he said, "The response is in there someplace." My first experience with neuroscience began during my first year in school. My most memorable school counsellor, Dr. Seymour Levine, an undeniably popular neuroendocrinologist, has directed spearheading work on the effect of stress during early life on the advancement of the cerebrum, which has moulded the entirety of my resulting thinking. His work assisted me in perceiving how early impacts can leave engraves on the mind that endures forever.

Levine had done a progression of trials inspecting the improvement of significant pressure-related chemical frameworks in rodents. His gathering's work showed that the science and capability of these significant frameworks could be changed decisively by brief times of pressure during early life.

Science isn't simply qualities playing out some unalterable content. It is touchy to its general surroundings, as developmental hypotheses anticipated. In a portion of the tests, the length of the pressure was just minutes long, including just a couple of seconds of human treatment of rodent little guys (child rodents), which is exceptionally distressing for them.

In any case, this exceptionally concise upsetting experience, at a critical time in the improvement of the cerebrum, brought about modifications in pressure chemical frameworks that endured into adulthood. From the second I began my proper schooling in the field, then, I was mindful of the extraordinary effect of early educational encounters.

This turned into a format against which I analysed every single ensuing idea. Habitually, while at the lab, my contemplations would go to Tina and the other kids with whom I was working.

I would compel myself to deal with the issue: What do I be aware of? Can anyone explain this? Could I at any point see any associations between what was known and what was not known? Was seeing me having any effect on the existence of these youngsters? As I naturally suspected about my patients,

I likewise viewed their side effects: Why these specific issues in this specific kid? What could assist with evolving them? Could their way of behaving be made sense of by anything that I and different researchers in my fields were finding out about how the cerebrum functions? For instance, could concentrating on the neurobiology of connection the association between parent

What's more, kids assist with taking care of issues between a mother and her child? Could Freudian thoughts like a transaction where a patient ventures his sentiments about his folks into different connections, especially the one he has with his advisor be made sense of by looking at the capability of the cerebrum?

There must be some connection, I thought. Since we were unable to portray it or on the other hand yet comprehend it, there just must be a connection between continued in the mind and each human peculiarity and side effect. All things considered, the human cerebrum is the organ that intercedes all inclination, thought, and conduct.

In contrast to other specific organs in the human body, like the heart, lungs and pancreas, the cerebrum is answerable for a large number of complex capabilities. At the point when you have a smart thought, experience passionate feelings for, tumble down the steps,

heave while strolling up steps, dissolve at the grin of your youngster, chuckle at a joke, get ravenous, and feel full those encounters and every one of your reactions to these encounters are intervened by your cerebrum. So it followed that Tina's battles with discourse and language, consideration, impulsivity, and solid connections, likewise needed to include her cerebrum.

In any case, which part of her cerebrum, and could understanding this assist me with treating her all the more successfully? Which of Tina's mind districts, brain organisations,furthermore, synapse frameworks were inadequately controlled, immature, or complicated, and what might this data do for me with Tina's treatment?

To address these inquiries I needed to begin with what I knew. The brain's Momentous useful abilities come from a similarly astounding arrangement of designs. There are 100 billion neurons (cerebrum cells), and for every neuron, there are ten similarly significant help cells, called glia. During improvement from the principal stirrings in the belly to early adulthood these muddled cells (and there are a large number of various sorts), should be coordinated into particular organisations.

These outcomes in incalculable, unpredictably interconnected and exceptionally particular frameworks. These chains and networks of associated neurons make the changed engineering of the mind.

For our motivations, there are four significant pieces of the mind: the brainstem, the diencephalon, the limbic framework, and the cortex. The mind is coordinated from back to front, similar to a house with progressively confounded increases based on an old establishment. The lower and most focal districts of the brainstem and the diencephalon are the easiest. They advance first, and They foster first as a youngster develops. As you move up and outward, things get progressively more complicated with the limbic framework.

The cortex is more complicated still, the unparalleled accomplishment of cerebrum design. We share the comparable association of our most minimal cerebrum areas with animals as crude as reptiles, while the centre districts are like those seen in vertebrates like a madhouse.

The external regions we share just with other primates, similar to monkeys and the extraordinary gorillas. The most exceptionally human part of the cerebrum is the cerebrum, however even this offers 96% of its association with that of a chimpanzee! Our four cerebrum regions are coordinated progressively: base to top, inside to outside. An effective method for imagining it is with a little pile of dollar bills, say five. Crease them into equal parts, put them on your palm, and make a drifter's clenched hand with your thumb calling attention to them.

Presently, turn your clenched hand in a "disapproval" direction. Your thumb addresses the brainstem, the tip of your thumb being where the spinal line converges into the brainstem; the greasy piece of your thumb would be the diencephalon; the collapsed dollars inside your clenched hand, covered by your fingers and hand, would be the limbic framework; What's more, your fingers and hands, which encompass the bills, address the cortex.

At the point when you take a gander at the human cerebrum, the limbic framework is inward; you can't see it from an external perspective, very much like those dollar greenbacks. Your little finger, which is presently arranged to be the top and front, addresses the cerebrum.

While interconnected, every one of these four principal regions controls a different set of capabilities. The brainstem, for instance, intercedes our centre's administrative works, for example, internal heat level, pulse, breath, and blood pressure.

The diencephalon and the limbic framework handle close-to-home reactions that guide our way of behaving, similar to fear, scorn, love, and euphoria. The very top piece of the mind, the cortex, manages the most intricate and profoundly human capabilities like discourse and language, theoretical reasoning, arranging, and conscious direction. Every one of them works in a show, similar to an ensemble symphony, so while there are individualised limits, nobody's framework is completely liable for the "music" you hear.

Tina's side effects proposed anomalies in practically each of the pieces of her mind. She had rest and consideration issues (brainstem), and challenges with fine engine control and coordination (diencephalon and cortex), clear friendly what's more, social deferrals and deficiencies (limbic and cortex) and discourse and language issues (cortex).

This unavoidable dissemination of issues was a vital sign. My research and the examination of many others showed that all of Tina's concerns could be connected with one critical arrangement of brain frameworks, the ones associated with assisting people with adapting to pressure and dangers. Incidentally, Those were the very frameworks I was concentrating on in the lab.

These frameworks were "suspect" to me for two fundamental reasons. The first was that, heap concentrates on people and creatures and reported the part these frameworks play in excitement, rest, consideration, hunger, mindset, and drive guideline every one of the areas where Tina had serious issues.

The second reason was that these significant organisations begin in the lower portions of the cerebrum and send direct associations with every one of the different regions of the mind. This design permits a one-of-a-kind job for these frameworks. They can incorporate and coordinate signs and data from our faculties in general furthermore, all through the mind. This limit is important to answer actually to a danger: if, for instance, a hunter is sneaking, a creature should be ready to answer similarly as fast to his aroma or sound as to see him.

Furthermore, the pressure reaction frameworks are among just a small bunch of brain frameworks in the mind that, if ineffectively controlled or strange, can cause brokenness in every one of the four principal cerebrum regions very much like how the situation was playing out with Tina.

The essential neuroscience work I'd been accomplishing for quite a long time involved looking at the subtleties of the way these functioned. In the mind, neurons send messages starting with one cell and then onto the next by utilising synthetic couriers called synapses that are delivered at specific neuron-to-neuron associations called neural connections.

These compound couriers fit exclusively into certain, accurately formed receptors on the following neuron, similar to that just the right key will squeeze into the lock on your front entryway.

Synaptic associations, immediately astoundingly complex but richly basic, make chains of neuron-to-neuron-to-neuron networks that permit numerous elements of the mind, including thought, feeling, feeling, sensation and discernment.

This additionally permits medications to influence us, because generally psychoactive prescriptions work like replicated keys, squeezing into the locks intended to be opened by specific synapses and tricking the cerebrum into opening or shutting their entryways.

I had done my doctoral examination in neuropharmacology in the lab of Dr. David U'Prichard, who had prepared with Dr. Solomon Snyder, a neuroscientist and therapist. (Dr. Snyder's gathering was well known for, among numerous different things, finding the receptor at which sedative medications like heroin furthermore, morphine acts.) When I worked with Dr. I explored the norepinephrine (otherwise called noradrenaline) and epinephrine (also known as adrenaline), frameworks.

These synapses are engaged with stress. The work of art "survival" reaction starts in a focal cluster of norepinephrine neurons known as the locus coeruleus ("blue spot," named for its tone). These neurons convey messages to essentially every other significant part of the mind and assist it with answering upsetting circumstances.

A portion of my work with Dr. U'Prichard involved two distinct kinds of rodents, which are creatures of the very species that had some slight hereditary contrasts. These rodents appeared to be identical in common circumstances, however, even the safest pressure would make one sort of break down.

Under quiet circumstances, these rodents could learn labyrinths, however, give them the littlest pressure, and they would unwind and fail to remember everything.

The other rodents were unaffected. At the point when we analysed their cerebrums, we viewed that as ahead of schedule in the advancement of the pressure-receptive rodents, there was over-action in their adrenaline and noradrenaline frameworks. This little change prompted an incredible fountain of irregularities in receptor number, awareness, and capability across many cerebrum regions, and eventually changed their capacity to respond appropriately to stress for a lifetime.

I had no proof that Tina was hereditarily "oversensitive" to push. I knew, notwithstanding, that the danger and the excruciating rapes Tina experienced had, most likely, brought about tedious and extreme enactment of Her alarming statement is intervening pressure reaction brain frameworks. I reviewed Levine's work that had shown that only a couple of moments of distressing experience right on time in life could change a rodent's pressure reaction until the end of time.

Tina's maltreatment had continued significantly longer; she'd been attacked no less than once every week for a considerable length of time and that had been intensified by the pressure of living in a consistent condition of emergency with a family that was in many cases on the financial edge. It seemed obvious to me that if the two qualities and climate could deliver comparative useless side effects, the impact of a distressing climate on an individual as of now hereditarily delicate to stress would presumably be amplified.

Also, as I kept on working both with Tina and in the lab, I came to trust that for Tina's situation the rehashed initiation of her pressure reaction frameworks from an injury persevered early on when her cerebrum was still creating had presumably caused a fountain of modified receptors, responsiveness furthermore, brokenness all through her cerebrum, like the one I saw in creature models. Thus, I began to believe Tina's side effects were the consequence of formative injury.

Her consideration and motivation issues may be because of an adjustment of the association of her pressure reaction brain networks, a change that could have once assisted her adapt to her maltreatment, however, it was presently making her forceful way of behaving and carelessness her class work in school.

It checked out: an individual with an overactive pressure framework would give close consideration to the essences of individuals like educators and schoolmates, where dangers could sneak, but not harmless things like homeroom examples.

An elevated familiarity with potential dangers could likewise make somebody like Tina inclined to battle, as she would look all over the place for signs that somebody may be going to go after her once more, probably causing her to blow up to the littlest expected signs of animosity.

This appeared to be a significantly more conceivable clarification for Tina's concerns than expected that her consideration issues were incidental and inconsequential to the maltreatment.

I thought back through her outline and saw that upon her most memorable visit to the centre, her pulse had been 112 beats each moment.

An ordinary pulse for a young lady of that age ought to have been under 100. A raised pulse can be a sign of a determinedly enacted pressure reaction, which was more proof of my thought that her concerns were an immediate consequence of her cerebrum reaction to the maltreatment. On the off chance that I needed to give Tina a name now, it wouldn't be ADD, but instead a post-horrible pressure problem, PTSD.

Over the three years I worked with Tina I was really glad and alleviated by her obvious advancement. There were no more reports of "unseemly" conduct at school. She was getting her work done, going to class, and battling with different kids. Her discourse had gotten to the next level; the greater part of her concerns had been connected with the way that she was so mild-mannered that educators and, surprisingly, her mom frequently couldn't hear her well enough to figure out her, not to mention right her elocution.

As she figured out how to make some noise and was addressed on a more regular basis, subsequently getting the rehashed restorative criticism she wanted, she got up to speed. She had likewise quickly become more mindful and less indiscreet, so quickly truth be told I didn't examine the prescription with my managers after that underlying discussion with Dr. Stine.

Tina directed our play during our meetings, however, I utilised each open door to show her illustrations that would help her vibe more certain out on the planet and also, assist her with acting all the more fittingly and objectively.

We at first learn drive control and decision-production from everyone around us, some of the time from unequivocal illustrations, in some cases as a visual demonstration. Tina, nonetheless, lived in a climate where neither unequivocal nor understood examples were instructed.

Everybody around her equally responded to what befell them, as that is what she did, as well. Our gatherings offered her the full focus she ached for and our games showed her a portion of the illustrations she had missed.

For the model, when I initially started my work with Tina she hadn't perceived the idea of alternating. She was unable to stand by to begin things, she acted and responded automatically. In the straightforward games that we played, I demonstrated a more proper way of behaving and over and again helped her to stop before doing the main thing that jumped into her head.

In light of her amazing advancement in school, I genuinely accepted I'd helped her. Unfortunately, fourteen days before I passed on the facility to begin a new position, presently ten-year-old Tina was found performing fellatio on a more seasoned kid at school. What I'd shown her, it appeared, was not to change her conduct, yet to all the more likely stow away her sexualized actions and different issues from grown-ups and to control her driving forces to try not to cause problems. On the surface, she could make others think she was acting properly, however inside, she had not conquered her injury.

I was Frustrated and confused after hearing this news. I had attempted so hard, and she was by all accounts improving. It was challenging to acknowledge that what appeared to be a positive remedial exertion had been so empty. What had occurred? Or then again more critically, what didn't occur in our work to assist with evolving her?

I continued to ponder the impacts Tina's youth injury and her temperamental home life might have had on her cerebrum. Before long I understood that I expected to extend my perspective on clinical psychological well-being work.

The responses to my fizzled, wasteful treatment for Tina and the unavoidable issues in kid psychiatry were in how the cerebrum functions, how the mind creates, how the cerebrum figures out and puts together the world. Not in that frame of mind as it has been satirised as an unbending, hereditarily, preset framework that occasionally expects drugs to change "uneven characters," however in the mind in all its Intricacy.

Not in that frame of mind as a fuming complex of oblivious "obstruction" and "disobedience," however in the cerebrum as it developed to answer a complex social world. A mind, so, that had hereditary inclinations that were moulded by development to be perfectly delicate to individuals who encircled it.

Tina improved her pressure framework; her better drive control appeared to be a great proof of this. In any case, Tina's generally alarming issues had to do with her misshaped and unfortunate sexual ways of behaving.

I understood that a portion of her side effects could be fixed by changing her overactive pressure reaction, yet that wouldn't delete her memory. I started to feel that memory was what I expected to comprehend before I could do better.

Anyway, what is memory? A large portion of us consider names, faces, and telephone numbers, however it is considerably more than that. It is a fundamental property of organic frameworks. Memory is the ability to convey forward in time some component of an encounter.

Indeed, even muscles have memory, as you can see by the progressions in them that outcome from working out. In particular, nonetheless, memory is what the mind does, how it forms us and permits our past to assist with deciding our future. By and large, memory makes us what our identity is and for Tina's situation, her recollections of sexual maltreatment were an enormous piece of what held her up.

Tina's bright and oversexualized connections with guys plainly originated from her maltreatment. I started thinking about memory and how the cerebrum makes "affiliations" when two examples of brain action happen at the same time and monotonously.

For instance, assuming the brain action caused by the visual picture of a fire engine and that brought about by an alarm co-happen redundantly, these once discrete brain chains (visual and sound related-brain organisations) will make new synaptic associations and become a single, interconnected network.

When this new arrangement of associations between visual and hear-able organisations are made, just invigorating one piece of the network (for instance, hearing the alarm) can actuate the visual part of the chain and the individual will consequently imagine a fire engine.

This strong property of affiliation is a general component of the cerebrum. It is through affiliation that we wind around our approaching tangible signs in general together with sound, sight, contact, fragrance to make the entire individual, place, thing, and activity. Affiliation permits and underlies both language and memory.

Our cognizant memory is brimming with holes which is a decent thing. Our minds sift through the conventional and expected, which is totally important to permit us to work. At the point when you drive, for instance, you depend consequently on your past encounters with vehicles and streets; assuming that you had to zero in on each part of what your faculties are taking in, you'd be overpowered and would likely crash.

As you learn anything, truth be told, your cerebrum is continually taking a look at current experience against putting away layouts basically memory of past, comparative circumstances and sensations, inquiring "Is this new?" and "Is this something I want to join in to?"

So as you drop not too far off, your cerebrum's engine vestibular framework lets you know that you are in a specific position. In any case, your mind is most likely not gaining new experiences about that.

Your cerebrum has put away its past sitting encounters in vehicles, and the example of brain action related to that doesn't have to change. There's the same old thing. You've been there, done that, it's recognizable. This is likewise why you can roll over enormous stretches of natural interstates without recalling nearly anything at all that you did during the drive.

This is significant because all of that recently put-away experience has laid down the brain organisations, the memory "format," that you currently use to figure out any new approaching data. These layouts are framed all through the mind at various levels, and because the data comes first to the lower, more crude regions, many are not indeed, even available to cognizant mindfulness.

For instance, youthful Tina nearly absolutely didn't know about the layout that directed her communications with men and significantly influenced her way of behaving with me when we initially met.

Further, we all have most likely had the experience of truly bouncing up before we even sorted out what it was that surprised us in any case. This occurs since our mind's pressure reaction frameworks convey data about likely dangers and are prepared to answer them as fast as could be expected, which frequently implies before the cortex can consider what move to make. If, like Tina, we have had profoundly upsetting encounters, tokens of those circumstances can be comparably strong and incite responses that are in basically the same manner driven by oblivious cycles.

What this likewise implies is that early encounters will fundamentally have a far more noteworthy effect than later ones. The cerebrum attempts to figure out the world by searching for designs. At the point when it joins reasonable, reliably associated designs together once more, it labels them as "typical" or "anticipated" and quits paying cognizant consideration. In this way, for instance, the absolute first time you were put in a sitting situation as a baby, you focused on the original sensations radiating from your hindquarters.

Your cerebrum figured out how to detect the strain related to sitting typically, you started to detect how to adjust your weight to sit upright through your engine vestibular framework and, ultimately, you figured out how to sit.

Presently, when you sit, except if it's awkward or the seat is surprisingly finished or formed or you have some sort of equilibrium issue, you give little consideration to remaining upstanding or the strain the seat puts on your back. At the point when you are driving, it's something you seldom go to by any means.

What you do filter the street for is curiosity, and awkward things, For example, a truck hurdling down some unacceptable side of the road. This is the reason we offload impressions of things we think about as ordinary: with the goal that we can quickly respond to unusual things and require prompt consideration.

Brain frameworks have advanced to be particularly delicate to curiosity since new encounters normally signal either risk or opportunity.

One of the main qualities of both memory, brain tissue, and improvement, then, at that point, is that they all change with designed, monotonous movement. In this way, the frameworks in your mind that get more than once will change and the frameworks in your cerebrum that don't get enacted won't change.

This "utilisation subordinate" improvement is perhaps the main property of brain tissue. It appears to be a straightforward idea, however it has colossal and boundless ramifications.

Understanding this idea, I came to accept, was vital to understanding youngsters like Tina. She had fostered an exceptionally lamentable set of affiliations since she was physically mishandled from the get-go throughout everyday life.

Her first encounters with men and her high school male victimizer formed her origination of which men are and the proper behaviour toward them; early encounters with people around us from all of our perspectives.

Because of the huge amount of data the cerebrum is defined with every day, we should use these examples to foresee what the world is like. Assuming early encounters are atypical, These expectations might direct our conduct in useless ways.

In Tina's world guys bigger than she was were startling, requesting animals who constrained her or her mom into sex. The fragrance, sight, and sounds related to them met up to make a set out of "memory layouts" that she used to get a handle on the world.

Thus, when she came into my office that first time and was separated from everyone else in the organisation of a grown-up male, it was completely normal for her to expect that I needed sex too. At the point when she went to class and uncovered herself or attempted to take part in a sex play with different youngsters, she displayed that she had some awareness of how to act. She didn't deliberately consider it.

It was only a bunch of ways of behaving that were essential for her harmful affiliations, her bent layout for sexuality. Tragically, with just an hour and seven days of treatment, it was nearly difficult to fix that arrangement of affiliations.

I could demonstrate the way of behaving of a different sort of grown-up male, I could show her that there were circumstances where sexual movement was improper and assisted her with figuring out how to stand up to motivations, however, I proved unable, in such a limited quantity of time, to supplant the format that had been manufactured in the new tissue of her young mind, that had been scorched in with a designed, tedious early experience.

I would have to coordinate much more about how the human cerebrum functions, how the mind changes and the frameworks that collaborate in this learning into my medicine before I actually might start to improve the situation for patients like Tina, patients whose lives and recollections had been damaged in more than one way by early injury.

Section 2

To Your Benefit

"I want your Assistance." The guest, Stan Walker,* was a lawyer for the Public Gatekeeper's office in Cook District, Illinois. I had finished my preparation in kid psychiatry and was currently an associate teacher at the College of Chicago, actually working at the facility and running my lab. It was 1990.

"I just acquired a case planned to go to preliminary one week from now," he told me, making sense of the fact that it was a crime. A three-year-old young lady named Sandy had seen the homicide of her mom. Presently, very nearly a year after the fact, the arraignment believed she should affirm it. "The fact that this may be makes me stressed overpowering for her," Stan went on, inquiring as to whether I could assist with setting her up for court.

"Overpowering?" I thought snidely to myself, "You think so?" Stan was a Watchman promotion litem, a lawyer selected by the court to address youngsters in the general set of laws. In Cook Area (where Chicago is found), the Public Watchman's Office uses its staff to address youngsters in the Kid Defensive Administrations (CPS) framework. In practically any remaining network this job is played by a named lawyer who may or may not have insight and preparation in kid regulation.

Cook Province had made the full-time positions with the honourable expectation that assuming the lawyers worked their cases full time, they could foster involvement in youngsters, find out about abuse, and in this manner better serve those they address. (Tragically, as with any remaining parts of the kid defensive framework, the volume of cases was overpowering and the workplace was underfunded.)

"Who is her specialist?" I asked, believing that somebody recognizable to the youngster would be a vastly better fit to assist her with getting ready. "She doesn't have one," he said. This was upsetting information. "No specialist? Where is she residing?" I inquired.

We don't have the foggiest idea. She is in child care yet the examiner and the Division of Youngster and Family Administrations is keeping her area undisclosed because there have been dangers to her life. She knew the suspect and distinguished him from the police. He is in a group and there is a contract out on her." This was sounding more regrettable and more awful.

"She gave a tenable ID at age three?" I inquired. I knew that onlooker declaration is effectively tested in court as a result of the properties of story memory we noted before, particularly its holes and how it tends to "fill in" the "normal." And from a four-year-old about an occasion that happened when she was three? On the off chance that the examiners didn't have some assistance, a decent protection lawyer would handily cause Sandy's declaration to show up as totally problematic.

"All things considered, she knew him," Stan made sense of, "She both immediately said he did it and later distinguished him from a photograph exhibit." I inquired as to whether there was any extra proof, feeling that perhaps a young lady's declaration wouldn't be vital. Assuming there was enough other proof, maybe I could assist him with persuading the examiner that affirming presented an extraordinary gamble of further damaging the kid. Stan made sense of that without a doubt.

Various kinds of actual proof set the culprit at the scene. Specialists had tracked down the young lady's mom's blood all around his garments. Regardless of having escaped the nation after carrying out the wrongdoing, the man had blood on his shoes at the point when he was captured.

"So for what reason does Sandy need to affirm?" I inquired. I was at that point beginning to feel pulled to help this kid. "That is essential for what we are attempting to sort out. We want to have the case delayed until we can either get her declaration by shut circuit Television or ensure she is prepared to affirm in court.

"He proceeded to portray the subtleties of the homicide, the young lady's hospitalisation because of wounds she'd got during the wrongdoing and her resulting child care situations.

As I tuned in, I discussed the choice of whether to reach out. To no one's surprise, I was overstretched and incredibly occupied. In addition, I'm awkward in court and I can't stand legal counsellors.

In any case, the more Stan talked, the more I was unable to trust what I was hearing. Individuals who should help this young lady from DCFS to the equity framework appeared to be ignorant regarding the impacts of injury on youngsters. I started to feel that she had the right to have somewhere around one individual in her life who probably wouldn't be.

"Thus, let me rehash this," I said, "A three-year-old young lady witnesses her mom being assaulted and killed. She has her throat cut, and two times, what's more, is left for dead. She is distant from everyone else with her dead mother's body for eleven hours in their loft.

Then, she's taken to the medical clinic and has the wounds on her neck treated. In the clinic, the doctors suggest continuous emotional well-being assessment and treatment. Be that as it may, after she's delivered, She's put in an encouraging home as a dependent of the government. Her CPS case manager

doesn't think she wants to see a psychological wellness proficient. Thus, notwithstanding the specialists' suggestions, he doesn't get her any assistance. For a considerable length of time, this youngster is moved from an encouraged home to a cultivated home with no direct or mental consideration at all.

The subtleties of the kid's encounters are never imparted to the temporary families since she is secluded from everything. Right?" "Better believe it, I surmise that is all obvious," he said, hearing the undeniable disappointment in my voice and how awful everything sounded when I depicted the circumstance so gruffly.

"What's more, presently, ten days before a homicide preliminary is booked to begin, you become mindful of the circumstance?" "Right," he conceded, timid at this point. "When did your office talk about this young lady?" I requested.

"We opened the case just after this occurred." "Nobody in your office remembered to guarantee that she had some psychological well-being support?" "We will more often than not survey situations when they come up for their hearings. We have many cases each." I wasn't amazed.

The public frameworks working with high-risk families and youngsters are overpowered. Strangely, during my long stretches of clinical preparation in youngster emotional wellness, I had close to nothing prologue to the kid defensive framework or the custom curriculum and adolescent equity frameworks, although over 30% of the kids coming to our centres were in at least one of these frameworks.

The compartmentalization of administrations, preparation, and perspectives was faltering. Also, I was learning, which is extremely disastrous for kids. When and where might I be at any point?" I inquired. I was unable to help myself.

I consented to meet Sandy in an office at the Court the following day. I was fairly astounded that Stan had called me for help. Before that This year he had sent me a "stop" letter.

In four long passages, I was informed that I should promptly legitimise the utilisation of a prescription called clonidine to "control" kids at a private treatment focus where I counselled.

I offered mental types of assistance to the youngsters in the middle. That's what the letter said on the off chance that I was unable to make sense of what I was doing, I should quickly stop this "trial" treatment. It was endorsed by Stan Walker in his authority limit as a lawyer with the Public Gatekeeper.

After accepting Stan's letter, I reached him to make sense of why I was utilising this medicine and why I accepted it would be an error to stop. The youngsters at this private place were among the state's generally troublesome cases. More than 100 young men had been put in this program; later "fizzling" encouraged homes because of serious conduct and mental issues.

Albeit the office acknowledged young men from seven to seventeen, the normal youngster in the office was a ten-year-old who had resided in ten earlier "homes," truly intending that for the greater part of them, no less than ten parent substitutes had thought that they were unmanageable.

Simple to work up and overpower however undeniably challenging to quiet down, these youngsters had been an issue for each guardian, specialist, and instructor they had experienced. At last, they'd get kicked out of cultivated homes, childcare settings, schools, and in some cases even treatment. The last stop was this middle.

After Looking into the records of exactly 200 young men who were then living in the middle or who had been there previously, I saw that every one of these young men no matter what had encountered extreme injury or misuse. By far most had somewhere around six significant horrendous encounters.

These kids had been naturally introduced to and raised with mayhem, danger, and injury. They were brooded in dread. Every one of them had been assessed on different occasions both previously and during their visit to the middle.

Each had been given many different DSM demonstrative marks, principally consideration deficiency/hyperactivity jumble, oppositional-disobedient turmoil, and lead problems very much like Tina.

Be that as it may amazingly, not very many of these kids were seen as "damaged" or "focused;" their injury wasn't considered applicable to analysis, similar to in Tina's case.

Despite extended narratives of aggressive behaviour at home, over and again hindered familial connections frequently including the deficiency of guardians to brutal demise or sickness, actual maltreatment, sexual maltreatment, and other predominantly upsetting occasions, few had been determined to have post-horrible pressure issues (PTSD).

PTSD didn't make it into the "differential determination," a rundown remembered for the case report of conceivable elective judgments with comparative side effects that every clinician considers, then, at that point, precludes.

Post-horrendous pressure problem was a somewhat new idea at that point, having been brought into the DSM analytic framework in 1980 to depict a condition tracked down in Vietnam veterans who, after getting back from their visits of obligation, frequently experienced tension, rest issues, and nosy and upsetting "flashback" recollections of occasions that occurred during the conflict.

They were oftentimes anxious and some answered forcefully to even the most minor signs of danger. Many had unnerving bad dreams and responded to uproarious clamours like they were discharged and they were still back in the wildernesses of Southeast Asia.

During my overall psychiatry preparation, I worked with vets who experienced PTSD. Numerous specialists were, and still, after all that, starting to perceive its commonness in grown-ups who'd experienced different sorts of awful encounters like assault and catastrophic events.

What struck me particularly was that, albeit the encounters that had scarred grown-ups with PTSD were frequently moderately short (generally going on for a couple of hours all things considered), their effect could still be found in their conduct years even many years later.

It reminded me of what Seymour Levine had tracked down in those rodent puppies, where a couple of moments Stress could change the mind forever. Should the effect of a horrendous encounter be for a kid!

Afterward, as an overall occupant in psychiatry, I concentrated on parts of the stress response frameworks in vets with PTSD. Different analysts and I viewed that as these veterans' pressure reaction frameworks were overactive, what researchers call "sharpened.

"This implied that when they were presented with minor Stressors and their frameworks responded like they were confronting incredible danger.

In a few cases, the mind frameworks related to the pressure reaction had turned out to be dynamic to such an extent that they in the long run "wore out" and lost their capacity to manage different capabilities they would ordinarily intercede.

Accordingly, the mind's ability to direct temperament, social connections, and unique discernment was likewise compromised. At the time I was working with the young men in the middle, I was proceeding to concentrate on the advancement of stress-related synapse frameworks in the lab.

I was looking at adrenaline and noradrenaline now, however investigating other related frameworks too: those utilising serotonin, dopamine furthermore, the endogenous narcotics, which are known as enkephalins and endorphins.

Serotonin is presumably most popular as the site of activity for stimulant prescriptions like Prozac and Zoloft; dopamine is known as the compound engaged with delight and inspiration engaged with the "high" from drugs like cocaine and amphetamine; endogenous narcotics are the cerebrum's regular pain relievers and are impacted by heroin, morphine, and comparable drugs.

These synthetic substances assume significant parts in the reaction to stretching, with adrenaline and noradrenaline setting up the body for survival, and dopamine gives a feeling of skill and the ability to accomplish one's objectives. Serotonin's activities are less simple to portray, however, the narcotics are known to mitigate, unwind, and decrease any aggravation that might be engaged with answering pressure and dangers.

After I'd perceived that Tina's consideration and impulsivity-related side effects were connected to a hyperarousal stress framework, I had started to think that meds that quieted the pressure framework could help other people like her.

Clonidine, an old and for the most part safe medicine, had for quite some time been used to treat individuals whose pulse was typically ordinary but soared into hypertension when they were under pressure. Clonidine made a difference in "calming" this reactivity down.

A fundamental report utilising this medicine had shown that it likewise helped decline PTSD-related hyper-excitement side effects in grown-up battle veterans. Knowing that the actual side effects a considerable lot of the young men at the private treatment community displayed were steady with an overactive, excessively receptive pressure framework, I chose to give clonidine a shot with their watchman's consent.

Furthermore, for some, it worked. Inside half a month of starting to take the drug, the young men's resting pulses had standardised and their rest moved along. Their consideration turned out to be more engaged and their impulsivity decreased.

Far superior, the young men's grades started to improve, as did their social communications with one another. As far as I might be concerned, this was nothing unexpected. By decreasing the overactivity in their pressure frameworks, the prescription empowered the young men to be less occupied by signs of danger.

This assisted them with becoming more mindful of both scholarly material and conventional meaningful gestures, permitting them to work on their homework and relational abilities (see Figure 3, Index, for extra subtleties).

I'd clarified all of this for Stan Walker after I'd gotten his letter. To my shock, he pulled out his protests and requested that I send him some more data about injury and youngsters. Tragically, as I informed him, there was very little composed on the point at that point. I sent him some of these early reports and some composing I had done myself. Until this call, I had not heard back from him.

The following day, as I arranged to meet Sandy, I attempted to envision the wrongdoing she'd seen according to her point of view. Nine months sooner she had been tracked down canvassed in blood, lying over her killed mother's bare body, crying disjointedly.

At the time she was not yet four. How should she go on, many days, with those pictures to her? How should I conceivably set her up for declaration, and the showdown of questioning, an undermining experience in any event, for grown-ups? What might she be like?

I likewise considered how she had endured mentally. How should her mind shield her from these horrendous encounters? What's more, how could any sensible individual, not to mention somebody prepared to manage upset kids, not understand that she wanted assistance after what she'd had to deal with?

Tragically, the overall perspective on kids and injury at that point, one that perseveres generally right up 'til now is that "kids are strong."

I visited the location of a homicide close to this time with a partner who had begun an injury reaction group to help people on the call to wrongdoing and mishap scenes. Police, paramedics, and firemen frequently see horrible scenes of death, mutilation, and decimation, and this can incur significant damage.

My partner was reasonably glad for the administrations he had been established to help these experts. As we strolled through the house where the casualty's blood doused the lounge chair and splattered the walls, I saw three small kids standing like zombies in the corner.

"Shouldn't something be said about the youngsters?" I asked as I gestured my head toward the three blood-dotted observers. He looked at them, thought briefly, and answered, "Youngsters are tough. They will be fine." Still youthful and deferential of my older folks, I gestured my head as though to recognize his insight. However, inside I was shouting.

Regardless, kids are more helpless against injury than grown-ups; I knew This was from Seymour Levine's work and crafted by many others by then. Strong youngsters are made, not conceived.

The creating mind is most pliant and generally delicate to encounter both great and awful right on time in life. (Therefore we with such ease and quickly learn the language, social subtlety, coordinated abilities, and many different things in adolescence, and why we talk about "developmental" encounters.) Kids become tough because of the examples of stress and sustenance that they experience from the get-go throughout everyday life, as We will see more meticulously later in this book.

Therefore, we are moreover quickly and handedly changed by injury when we are young. However, its impacts may not generally be apparent to the undeveloped eye, when, guess what injury can do to kids, tragically, you start to see its consequences all over.

Around then my research facility was concentrating on neurobiological instruments, which I knew were connected with strength and weakness to push. We were looking at an inquisitive yet vital impact of medications that invigorate the frameworks I'd been concentrating on in the cerebrum. These impacts are called refinement and resistance, and they have significant ramifications for understanding the human psyche and its response to injury.

In refinement, an example of improvement prompts expanded aversion to future comparative improvements. This is found in the Vietnam veterans and the rodents that were hereditarily oversensitive to push or turned into that way because of early openness to it.

At the point when the mind becomes sharpened, even little Stressors can incite huge reactions. Resilience, going against the norm, quiets one's reaction to an encounter after some time. The two elements are significant for the working of memory: if we don't get open-minded toward recognizable encounters, they will constantly show up new and possibly overpowering. The mind would presumably run out of capacity limit, similar to an old PC.

Also, on the off chance that we didn't turn out to be progressively delicate to specific things, we wouldn't have the option to further develop how we answer them. Inquisitively, the two impacts can be accomplished with a similar measure of the same medication, however, you obtain inverse outcomes assuming that the example of medication use is unique. For instance, if a rodent, or a human, is given little, incessant portions of medications like cocaine or heroin that follow up on the dopamine and narcotic frameworks, the medications lose their "strength.

This is important for what occurs during compulsion: the fiend becomes lenient, thus a greater amount of the medication is expected to accomplish something very similar "high." Interestingly, on the off chance that you give a creature the equivalent day-to-day amount of medication, however in enormous, rare portions, the medication in fact "gains" strength.

In two weeks a portion that caused a gentle response on day one can cause a significant and delayed eruption on day fourteen. Sharpening to medication, at times, can prompt seizures and indeed, even demise, a peculiarity that might be liable for some in any case incomprehensible medication glutes.

Tragically for junkies, their medication hankering tends to produce examples of purpose that prompt resilience, not sharpening to the "high" that they want, while at the same time creating refinement to certain bothersome impacts, similar to the suspicion related to cocaine use.

All the more significantly, our motivations, versatility, or weakness to push relies on an individual's brain framework's resilience or refinement following prior encounters. These impacts can likewise help further make sense of the distinction between stress and injury, which is essential to comprehend as we consider kids like Tina and Sandy. For instance, "Put it to work, or it will quit working for you" is something we hear at the exercise centre understandably.

Idle muscle gets powerless, while dynamic muscle gets more grounded. This guideline is alluded to as "use dependence." Likewise, the more a framework in the cerebrum is enacted, the more that framework will fabricate or keep up with synaptic associations.

The progressions of memory of sorts in muscle happen because designed, dull movement conveys a message to muscle cells that "you will work at this level" so they roll out the sub-atomic improvements expected to accomplish that work without any problem. To change the muscle, in any case, the redundancies should be designed.

Twisting 25 pounds multiple times in three firmly planned sets of ten twists prompts more grounded muscle. Assuming you twist 25 pounds multiple times indiscriminately during the day, be that as it may, the sign to the muscle is conflicting, tumultuous, and deficient to make the muscle cells become more grounded. Without the example, the same redundancies and the very same all-out weight will create an undeniably less compelling outcome.

To make a viable "memory" and increment strength, the experience must be designed. What's more, it's dull. Thus it is with the neurons, brain frameworks, and the cerebrum. Examples of experience matters. On a cell-by-cell premise, no other tissue is more fit to change in light of designed dreary signs. Without a doubt, neurons are intended to do precisely that. This subatomic gift permits memory.

It produces the synaptic associations that permit us to eat, type, have intercourse, play b-ball, and do all the other things a person can do.

It is this unpredictable snare of interconnection that makes the mind work. By driving either your muscles or your cerebrum to work, notwithstanding, you do "stress" them. Organic frameworks exist in balance. To work they need to remain inside a specific restricted range fitting to their current action, and the mind is accused of keeping up with this fundamental Harmony.

The experience is a stressor; the effect on the framework is stress. Thus, assuming you get dried out during exercise, for instance, that stress will make you parched because your mind is attempting to drive you to supplant the required liquids. Essentially, when a youngster learns another jargon word, there is a small pressure applied to the cortex, which requires a redundant feeling to make a precise review.

Without the pressure, the framework wouldn't realise there is a novel, new thing to take care of. All in all, stress isn't continuously awful. To be sure, if moderate, unsurprising, and designed, stress makes a framework more grounded and all the more practically competent.

Subsequently, the more grounded muscle in the present is the one that has gotten through moderate pressure previously. What's more, The equivalent is valid for the mind's pressure reaction frameworks. Through moderate, Unsurprising difficulties our pressure reaction frameworks are initiated reasonably.

This makes for a tough, adaptable pressure reaction limit. The more grounded stress reaction framework in the present is the one that has had moderate, designed pressure before. Nonetheless, that isn't the entire story.

On the off chance that you attempt to seat press 200 beats on your most memorable outing to the exercise centre, assuming you truly do figure out how to lift the load at all, you're not liable to assemble muscle, yet tear it and hurt yourself.

The example and power of involvement matter. On the off chance that a framework is over-burden worked past the limit the outcome can be significant decay, complication and brokenness whether you are exhausting your back muscles at the exercise centre or your mind's pressure networks when stood up to with awful pressure.

This likewise intends that because of the fortifying impact of past moderate and designed encounters, what might be upsetting for one individual might be minor for another. Similarly, as a muscle head can convey loads that undeveloped individuals couldn't move, so too can a few minds manage horrible mishaps that would injure others.

The specific situation, timing, and reaction of others matter significantly. The demise of a parent is undeniably more horrendous for the two-year-old offspring of a single parent than it is for a fifty-year-old wedded man with offspring of his own.

For Tina's situation and that of the young men in the middle, their experience of pressure was a long way past their young frameworks' abilities to convey it. As opposed to moderate, unsurprising, and fortifying actuation of their pressure frameworks, they had experienced flighty, delayed, and outrageous encounters that had denoted their young lives significantly.

I was unable to see a way that this wouldn't be valid for Sandy also. Previously I met him. I attempted to get as much foundation and history on Sandy as I could. I conversed with her ongoing temporary family, her new case manager, and, eventually, with individuals from her more distant family.

I learned that she had significant rest issues and was unavoidably restless. I was informed that she had an expanded frightened reaction. Very much like the damaged Vietnam vets I'd worked with, she would hop at the smallest unforeseen clamour. She likewise had verbose times of staring off into space, during which it was very hard to get her to "wake up."

A specialist without realising her set of experiences could have determined her to have the "nonattendance" or on the other hand "petit mal" type of epilepsy: she was that difficult to reach during these episodes.

I additionally discovered that Sandy now and again had forceful, fit-like eruptions. Her temporary family couldn't track down any example of these ways of behaving, and also, couldn't pinpoint what set them off. Yet, they revealed one more arrangement of "odd" ways of behaving: Sandy would have rather not utilised flatware.

She was particularly scared of blades; yet she additionally would not drink milk, or even look at milk bottles. At the point when the doorbell rang, she would conceal herself like a sketchy feline, once in a while so really that it required twenty minutes for her temporary parents to see her.

She could likewise be found, once in a while, concealing under a bed, behind a sofa, in a cupboard under the kitchen sink, shaking and crying. So much for strength.

Sandy's frightened response alone let me know that her stress-reaction frameworks had become sharpened. Affirming would drench her in difficult tokens of that horrendous evening. I needed to get some feeling of whether she could endure it.

However, I would have rather not, sooner or later in my underlying visit I must test her memory a little to see how she would respond. In any case, I support myself with the information that a little torment currently could assist with safeguarding her from a great deal of agony later, and may indeed, even assist her in starting the mending system.

I Initially met Sandy in a little room housed in a normal, clean government building. It had been set up to be "kid amicable" with some youngster-size furniture, toys, pastels, shading books, and paper.

A couple of animation figures had been painted on the walls, however, "framework" actually shouted out from the tile floors and soot block development. At the point when I strolled in, Sandy was sitting on the floor with certain dolls around her. She was shading. What first struck me, as it had when I initially met Tina, was how little she was.

I estimated She stood a piece under four feet tall. She had tremendous, fluid earthy coloured eyes and long, thick, wavy coloured hair. On her neck were noticeable scars on the two sides, from her ears to the centre of her throat. However, they were substantially less observable than I had envisioned they might be; the plastic specialists had done steady employment.

As I strolled in with Stan she quit all that and gazed at me, frozen. Stan presented me. "Sandy, this is the specialist I filled you in about. He is going to converse with you, alright?" he asked restlessly. She didn't move, not one millimetre.

There was no adjustment of her careful articulation. Accordingly, Stan took a gander at me and back at her gave a major grin, and said in his best lively, kindergarten-instructor voice, "Alright. Great. All things considered, I will leave both of you together." As he left I saw him like he was nuts, shocked by how he'd excused Sandy's absence of reaction to his inquiry. At the point when I glanced back at Sandy, her face wore the very appearance that mine did.

I shook my head, shrugged my shoulders, and gave a little grin. As though in a reflection, Sandy did likewise. Aha! An association! This was a decent beginning, I thought. Try not to neglect it away.

I knew whether I strolled toward this minuscule young lady. I'm quite enormous here. A sharpened alert reaction would go off the deep end. Her environmental elements were at that point Adequately new, new grown-ups, new spot, new circumstance. I wanted her to remain as quiet as could be expected.

"I need a variety as well," I said without checking her out. I needed to be however unsurprising as could be expected and told her what I might have been going to do in the aerobics step.

No unexpected moves. Make yourself more modest, I thought, get on the floor.

Try not to see her, don't confront her, and utilise slow intentional developments as you variety. I plunked down on the floor, a couple of feet away. I attempted to make my voice as relieving and quiet as could be expected.

"I like red. This ought to be a red vehicle," I expressed, pointing at an image in my shading book. Sandy concentrated all over, my hands, and my sluggish developments. She was simply part of the way, mindful of my words. This young lady was legitimately dubious.

For quite a while, I hued alone, prattling about my selections of varieties, being all around as relaxed and amicable as conceivable without being excessively "brilliant" as Stan had been the point at which he attempted to veil his uneasiness. In the end, Sandy broke the musicality by pushing a piece nearer toward me and quietly guiding me to utilise a particular tone, I consented.

When she approached me, I stopped talking. For the overwhelming majority of minutes more we shaded together peacefully. I still couldn't seem to get some information about what had occurred, yet I could detect that she realised for that reason I was there and that she realised that I realised she knew.

Each of the grown-ups in her "new" life had eventually, somehow or another returned her to that evening. "What befell your neck?" I asked, highlighting her two scars. She went about as though she didn't hear me. She didn't change her demeanour.

She did indeed not change the speed of her shading. I rehashed the inquiry. Presently, she froze. Shading halted. Her eyes gazed vacantly at nothing in particular, unblinking. Once more, I asked. She took her pastel and wrote over her very much-shaped, restrained picture however gave no reaction.

Once more, I inquired. I couldn't stand this. I realised I was pushing her toward her excruciating recollections. Sandy stood up, snatched a stuffed hare, held it by the ears, and sliced at the neck of the creature with the coloured pencil. As she cut, she rehashed, "It's for your great, fella." Again and again a stuck recording.

She tossed the creature to the floor, hurried to the radiator, moved up, and leaped off over and over. She didn't answer my admonitions to be cautious. Stressed that she would hurt herself, I rose and got her on one of her leaps. She softened into my arms. We sat together for a couple of minutes. Her excited breathing eased back and afterward practically halted.

And afterward, in a sluggish, automated droning she enlightened me concerning that evening. An associate of her mom had come to their loft. He had rang the doorbell and her mom had given him access. "Mother was shouting, the troublemaker was hurting her," she said. "I ought to have killed him."

"At the point when I emerged from my room and mom was snoozing, then, at that point, he cut me," she proceeded, "He expressed, 'It's for your great, fella.'" The aggressor had slit her jugular two times. Sandy quickly fell.

Afterward, she recovered awareness and endeavoured to "awaken" her mom. She took milk from the cooler and choked when she attempted to drink some. It overflowed through the cut in her throat. She attempted to give some to her mother, however, "she was not parched," Sandy told me.

That's what Sandy meandered in the loft for eleven hours before anybody came. A family member stressed that Sandy's mom had not picked up the telephone, had come around, and found a frightening crime location.

By the Finish of that interview, I was sure that affirming would be destroying Sandy. She wanted assistance and, assuming she needed to affirm, more time to get ready. Stan would work effectively, as it ended up, to delay the preliminary. "Might you at some point do the treatment?" he asked me. Obviously. I proved unable to say no.

The images of Sandy consumed into my psyche during that meeting were faltering: a three-year-old youngster, her throat cut, sobbing, attempting to solace and looking for solace from her stripped mother's hoard-tied, ridiculous, and at last virus body.

How powerless, confounded, and alarmed she probably felt! Her side effects, her "nonattendances," her avoidant reactions to my inquiries, her stowing away, and her particular feelings of trepidation were guards developed by her mind to keep the injury under control. Understanding those safeguards would be basic to assisting her and different kids with enjoying her.

Indeed, even in utero and after birth, for each snapshot of every day, our cerebrum is handling the relentless arrangement of approaching signs from our faculties. Sight, sound, contact, smell, taste every one of the crude tactile information that will result in these sensations enter the lower portions of the cerebrum and start a multistage interaction of being arranged, contrasted with recently put away examples, and eventually, if essential, followed up on.

By and large, the example of approaching signs is so tedious, so recognizable, so protected and the memory layout that this example matches is so profoundly engrained, that your mind overlooks them. This is a type of resistance called adjustment.

We disregard recognizable examples in conventional settings, to such an extent that we disregard huge segments of our days, which are spent doing routine things like cleaning our teeth or getting dressed.

We'll recollect whether a natural example happens inappropriately, in any case. For example, you may be on a setting up camp excursion, cleaning your teeth as the sun comes up. The magnificence existing apart from everything else is strong to the point that you will recollect this one time as a novel. Feelings are strong markers of setting.

The joy and delight of the dawn in this occurrence is uncommon in the "brushing teeth" memory format, so it makes it more distinctive and important. Likewise, on the off chance that you end up cleaning your teeth when a seismic tremor annihilates your home, those occasions might turn out to be everlastingly associated in your mind and reviewed together.

Pessimistic feelings frequently make things considerably more critical than positive ones because reviewing things that are undermining also, staying away from those circumstances later on if conceivable is frequently basic to endurance.

A mouse that didn't figure out how to keep away from the fragrance of felines after one terrible experience, for instance, wouldn't be a mouse liable to create a large number of posterity. Subsequently, in any case, such affiliations can turn into the wellspring of injury-related side effects.

For a quake survivor who was brushing her teeth when the house imploded around her, just seeing a toothbrush may be sufficient to incite an undeniable trepidation reaction.

For Sandy's situation, milk, once connected with sustaining and sustenance, presently turned into the stuff that spilled from her throat, that her mom "declined" as She lay dead. Flatware was currently not generally something used to eat your food, but rather something that killed and harmed and astonished.

What's more, doorbells indeed began the entire thing: the ringing of the doorbell had reported the appearance of the executioner.

For her purposes, these everyday and customary things had become suggestive signs that kept her in a condition of ceaseless trepidation. This befuddled her encouraged guardians and her educators, who didn't have the foggiest idea about the subtleties of what had occurred to her and consequently frequently couldn't perceive what may be inciting her bizarre way of behaving.

They couldn't comprehend the reason why she would be so sweet one second and afterward hasty, disobedient, and forceful the following. The eruptions appeared to be detached from any occasion or collaboration that the grown-ups could distinguish. Yet, both the appearance of unconventionality and the idea of her ways of behaving appeared to be legit. Her cerebrum was attempting to safeguard her based on what it had recently found out about the world.

The cerebrum is continuously contrasting current approaching examples and putting away formats and affiliations. This matching system happens at first in the least, most straightforward pieces of the cerebrum, where, as you might review, the brain frameworks associated with answering dangers begin.

As the data moves up from this first phase of handling, the cerebrum has chances to require another glance at the information for more intricate thought and coordination. In any case, from the beginning, all it needs to know is: Does this approaching information possibly proposing risk? If the experience is natural and known as protected, the cerebrum's pressure framework won't be enacted.

Be that as it may, assuming that the approaching data is at first new, new, or unusual, the mind quickly starts a pressure reaction. How widely these pressure frameworks are initiated is connected with how compromising the circumstance shows up. It's essential to comprehend that our default is set at doubt, not acknowledgment.

At the very least, when confronted with new and obscure examples of action, we become more ready. The mind's objective at this point is to get more data, look at the circumstance, and decide just how perilous it may be. Since people have forever been the deadliest creature experienced by different people, we intently screen nonverbal signs of human threats, like manner of speaking, look, and body language.

Upon additional assessment, our cerebrum might perceive that the new example of Actuation has been brought about by something recognizable, yet wrong. For example, on the off chance that you are in the library perusing and somebody drops a weighty book on a table, the noisy clamour will quickly make you quit perusing.

You will initiate your excited reaction, centre around the wellspring of the commotion, and order it as a protected, natural mishap may be irritating, yet nothing to stress about. If, then again, you hear a boisterous clamour in the library, turn, and find that others around you appear to be frightened, then, at that point, turn upward and see a man with a weapon, your cerebrum would move from excitement to caution and most likely then into all-out dread.

Assuming shortly, you discover that this was a terrible understudy trick, your mind would gradually drop down this excitement continuum toward a condition of quiet. The apprehension reaction is reviewed, and adjusted by the cerebrum's apparent degree of danger (see Figure 3, Informative supplement).

As you become progressively terrified, the danger frameworks in your cerebrum keep on coordinating approaching data and organise a complete body reaction pointed toward keeping you alive.

Keeping that in mind, a noteworthy arrangement of associating brain and hormonal frameworks cooperate to ensure your cerebrum and the remainder of your body do the right things. To begin with, your mind makes you quit contemplating insignificant things by closing down the prattle of the cerebrum.

Then, at that point, it centres around signals from others around you to assist you with figuring out who could safeguard or undermine you, by letting the limbic framework's "meaningful gesture perusing" frameworks dominate.

Your pulse increments to get blood to your muscles on the off chance that you want to battle or escape. Your muscle tone additionally increments and sensations like yearning are put aside. In a huge number of various ways, your cerebrum plans to safeguard you.

At the point when we are quiet it is not difficult to live in our cortex, utilising the most elevated limits of our minds to mull over deliberations, make arrangements, long for the future, and read.

Yet, assuming something stands out for us and meddles with our considerations, we become more cautious and concrete, moving the equilibrium of our cerebrum action to subcortical regions to elevate our faculties to identify dangers.

As we push up the excitement continuum toward dread, then, at that point, we essentially depend on lower and quicker cerebrum locales. In a complete frenzy, for model, our reactions are reflexive and under basically no cognizant control. Dread makes us stupider, a property that permits quicker responses in brief periods and helps quick endurance.

In any case, dread can become maladaptive on the off chance that it is maintained; the danger framework becomes sharpened to continually keep us in this state. This "hyper-excitement" reaction represented a significant number of Sandy's side effects.

In any case, not every one of them. The cerebrum doesn't have only one bunch of variations for danger. In the circumstance Sandy confronted she was so little and thus frail and the danger she encountered was overpowering to the point that she couldn't battle or escape.

Assuming her cerebrum had answered by raising her pulse and setting up her muscles for activity, that would just have made her bound to drain to passing when she was harmed. Incredibly, our cerebrums have a bunch of transformations for these sorts of circumstances too, which represents another significant arrangement of injury-related side effects, known as "dissociative" reactions.

Separation is an extremely crude response: the earliest living things (and the most youthful individuals from higher species) can seldom get away from critical circumstances under their own steam. Their main conceivable reaction to being gone after or harmed, then, at that point, is basically to twist up, make themselves as little as could be expected, sob for help, and expectation for a marvel.

This reaction gives off an impression of being driven by the most crude mind frameworks, situated in the brainstem and right away encompassing it. For babies and small kids, unequipped for or incapable of battling or escaping, a dissociative reaction to outrageous stressors is normal.

It is additionally more normal in females than guys and, whenever delayed, separation is associated with expanded chances for post-horrendous pressure side effects.

During separation, the mind readies the body for injury. Blood is shunted away from the appendages and the pulse eases back to diminish blood misfortune from wounds. A surge of endogenous narcotics the mind's regular heroin-like substances is delivered, killing torment, and creating quiet and a feeling of mental separation based on what's going on.

Like the hyper-excitement reaction, the dissociative reaction is reviewed and happens on a continuum. Standard states like wandering off in fantasy land and advances Among rest and alertness are gentle types of separation. A mesmerising Daze is another model.

In outrageous dissociative encounters, notwithstanding, the individual turns out to be centred internally and detached from reality. Mind areas that rule figuring shift from arranging activity to worrying about beast endurance. There is a feeling that time has eased back and what's going on isn't "genuine." Breathing eases back. Agony and even dread shut down. Individuals frequently report feeling deadpan and numb, as however they are watching what's befalling them influence a person in a film.

In most horrible encounters, in any case, not one however a mix of These two significant reactions happen. Without a doubt, generally speaking, a moderate separation during a horrendous mishap can balance the power and terms of the hyper-excitement reaction.

The ability to turn into "numb" and to some degree automated during battle, for instance, permits the officer to proceed to work really without alarm. Be that as it may, now and again, one example or the other prevails. Assuming that these examples are initiated more than once lengthy enough, because of the power, term, or example of the injury, there will be ASAP "use-subordinate" changes in the brain frameworks that intercede these reactions.

The outcome is that these frameworks can become overactive and sharpened, prompting a large group of profound, conduct, and mental issues long after the horrible mishap is finished. We have come to comprehend that many post-awful mental side effects are connected with either dissociative or hyper-excitement reactions to recollections of the injury.

These reactions can help individuals endure prompt injury, however, if they persevere, they can cause serious issues in different everyday issues not too far off. There are not many better instances of injury-related issues than what I found in those young men in the private community. The effect of injury and the continuous error of its side effects uncovered itself in the way that virtually all of them had some sort of determination connected with consideration Furthermore, direct issues.

In a study hall setting, tragically, both separation and hyper-excitement reactions seem to be considered shortage confusion, hyperactivity, or oppositional-insubordinate turmoil. Separated kids are not focusing: they appear to be fantasising or "scattering," as opposed to zeroing in on homework, and to be sure, they have blocked out their general surroundings.

Hyper-stimulated youth can look hyperactive or oblivious because what they are taking care of is the educator's manner of speaking or the other kids' non-verbal communication, not the content of their examples.

The hostility and impulsivity that the instinctive reaction incites can likewise show up as rebellion or resistance, when it is the remainders of a reaction to some earlier horrendous circumstance that the youngster has in some way or another been incited to review. The "freezing" reaction that the body makes when focused on unexpected stability, similar to a deer trapped in the headlights, is moreover frequently confounded as a resistant refusal by educators since, when it happens, the kid in a real sense can't answer orders.

While not all ADD,hyperactivity and oppositional-disobedient confusion are injury related, it is reasonable that the side effects that lead to these judgments are injury-related surprisingly frequently. When I first met Sandy for treatment, it was in the hall of a congregation.

In any case, in a type of witness security, she must be shielded from the executioner's kindred gangsters, who couldn't be captured because they hadn't straightforwardly participated in the wrongdoing. So we met in uncommon spots at abnormal times. Frequently, this ended up being Sundays at a congregation.

She was there with her non-permanent parents. I welcomed them. Sandy remembered me however did not grin. I carried her temporary mother into the room where we were to hold the meeting, a preschool study hall. Then, at that point, I took a few pastels and paper and set them down on the rug to variety.

In a little while Sandy came over and went along with me on the floor. I glanced over to the non-permanent mother and said, "Sandy, Mrs. Sally will go to the chapel while we play. Is that alright?" She didn't turn upward, however, she said, "Alright."

We sat on the floor and shaded peacefully. For ten minutes our play was very much like the underlying visit to the court. Then, at that point, it changed. Sandy halted shading. She took the pastel from my hand, pulled at my arm, and pulled at my shoulder to make me lay face down on the floor.

"What game is this?" I asked energetically. "No. Try not to talk," she said. She was dangerous, difficult and powerful. She had me twist my knees and put my arms despite my good faith as though I was hoard tied. And afterward, the reenactment occurred. For the following forty minutes, she meandered the study hall, murmuring things, just some of which I heard.

"This is great. You can eat this," she expressed, approaching me with plastic vegetables and opening my mouth to attempt to take care of me. Then, at that point, she brought a cover over to cover me. During that underlying treatment meeting, she would move toward me, lay on me, shake me, open my mouth and my eyes, and afterward leave again to track down something in the room, quite often getting back with a toy or another item.

She didn't reenact her attack, and for the rest of the time I worked with her she never did completely reenact it, however, she habitually said, "For your great, fella," as she strolled around. While she did this, I needed to do precisely the exact thing she needed: don't talk, don't move, don't meddle, don't stop. She expected to have complete control while she played out this reenactment.

What's more, that control, I started to perceive, would be basic to assisting her with mending. All things considered, one of the characterising components of a horrible encounter, especially one that is horrendous to such an extent that one separates since there is no alternate method for getting away from it is a finished loss of control and a feeling of absolute frailty.

Therefore, recovering control is a significant part of adapting to horrendous pressure. This should be visible strikingly in the exemplary exploration of a peculiarity that has come to be known as "learned powerlessness."

Martin Seligman and his associates at the College of Pennsylvania made this trial worldview in which two creatures (for this situation, rodents) are housed in discrete yet contiguous enclosures. In one of these enclosures, each time the rodent presses a switch to get food, it is first given an electric shock.

This is, obviously, unpleasant for the rodent, however over the long haul, perceiving that it will get food after the shock, it changes and becomes lenient. The rodent knows that the possible time it will be stunned is the point at which it presses the switch, so it has some degree of command over the circumstance.

As we've examined, over the long haul, an unsurprising and controllable stressor causes less "stress" on the framework while resilience increases. Yet, in the subsequent enclosure, while the rodent can press the bar to get food just like the rodent in the principal enclosure does, this one gets stunned when the other rodent presses the switch.

As such, the subsequent rodent has no clue about when it will be stunned and had zero influence over the circumstance. This rodent becomes sharpened to the stress, not acclimated to it. In the two rodents, significant changes should be visible in the stress frameworks of their minds: solid changes on account of the rodents with command over the pressure, and disintegration and dysregulation in the others.

The creatures that don't have command over the shock frequently foster ulcers, get thinner and have compromised safe frameworks that make them more powerless to illness. Tragically, in any event, when the circumstance is changed so they have some control over the shock, creatures that have been put in a circumstance without control for quite some time become too scared to even think about investigating the enclosure to sort out some way to help themselves.

A similar sort of debilitation and acquiescence can frequently be found in people who become discouraged, and research progressively interfaces the gamble of despondency to the number of wild distressing occasions individuals experience during their youth. PTSD is as often as possible joined by despondency.

Because of the connection between control and adjustment, and between the need of control and refinement, recuperation from injury expects that the person in question gets back to a circumstance that is unsurprising and safe. Our minds are normally pulled to figure out injury in a manner that permits us to become open-minded of it, to intellectually move the horrendous experience from one in which we are powerless to one in which we have some authority.

That is the thing Sandy was doing in her reenactment conduct. She controlled our communications such that permitted her to "titrate" the level of pressure during the meetings. Like a specialist adjusting the ideal impacts and incidental effects of medication by picking the right portion, Sandy directed her openness to the stress of her reenactment play.

Her mind was pulling her to make a more passable example of stress; a more unsurprising encounter that she could put in its place and abandon. Her cerebrum was trying, through reenactment, to make the injury into something unsurprising, and ideally, eventually exhausting. Example and redundancy are the keys to this. Designed, redundant upgrades lead to resistance, while tumultuous, rare signs produce sharpening.

To reestablish its balance, the cerebrum attempts to calm our sharpened, injury-related recollections by pushing us to have redundant, little "dosages" of review. It tries to create a sharpened framework to foster resilience. What's more, by and large, This works.

In the prompt fallout of a troubling or horrendous mishap we have meddling contemplations: we continue to ponder what occurred, we dream about it, we wind up contemplating it when we would rather not, and what's more, we frequently tell and retell the occasion to confide in companions or friends and family.

Youngsters will reenact the occasions in the play, drawings, and their day-to-day connections. The more extreme and overpowering the experience, nonetheless, the harder it becomes to "desensitise" all of the injury-related recollections. In her reenactments with me, Sandy was endeavouring to foster resistance to her awful horrendous recollections.

She had control of these reenactments; This control allows her to tweak her degree of misery. Assuming it turned out to be as well extreme she could divert our play, and that is the very thing that she frequently did. I didn't attempt to disrupt the interaction or push her to review anything after the first time when I needed to do it for the assessment.

In the main months of our work together every meeting would begin the same way: quietly. She would reach up for my hand and lead me to the centre of the room, pull me down, and signal. I would sit down and twist myself into the hoard-tied position. She would investigate the room, return what's more, and forward it to me. At long last, she would come and lay on my back.

She would begin to murmur discreetly and rock. I had some better sense than not to talk or change position. I let her have the all-out control she wanted. It was lamentable. The reactions of damaged youngsters are frequently misconstrued.

This even happened to Sandy at certain places in childcare. Since new circumstances are intrinsically unpleasant, and because young people who have experienced injury frequently come from homes in which turmoil and eccentrics show up "ordinary" to them, they might answer with dread to what is a quiet and safe circumstance.

Endeavouring to assume command over what they accept is the unavoidable return of tumult, they seem to "incite" it to cause things to feel more agreeable and unsurprising. Subsequently, the "special night" time frame in cultivated care will end as the kid acts resistant and disastrously to brief natural shouting and cruel discipline.

Like every other person, they feel more alright with what is "natural." As one family specialist broadly put it, we will generally favour the "conviction of hopelessness to the wretchedness of vulnerability." This reaction to an injury can frequently create difficult issues for youngsters when it is gotten by their overseers wrong.

Luckily, in this situation, I had the option to teach the people who worked with Sandy about what's in store and how to answer it. Yet at the same time, beyond treatment, at first her rest, uneasiness, and social issues continued to happen. Her resting pulse was north of 120, very high for a young lady her age.

Notwithstanding intermittent significant dissociative ways of behaving, she was probably going to show up "tuned up" and hyper-cautious comparable, here and there, to the young men I was seeing in the private place. I examined the possible constructive outcomes of clonidine with her temporary family, her case manager, and with Stan.

They concurred that we ought to attempt it and, to be sure, her rest before long improved and the recurrence, force, and span of her complete implosions diminished. She began to be more straightforward to reside with and to educate, at home as well as in her preschool study hall.

Our treatment went on too. After around twelve meetings she began to change the situation in which she believed that I should lie. No seriously being pig-tied; presently I would lie on my side. A similar custom occurred. She investigated the room, continuously returning to my body lying on the floor and presenting to me the things she had gathered.

She would in any case hold my head to attempt to feed me. And afterward, she'd rest on me, shaking, murmuring parts of tunes, here and there halting as though frozen. Here and there, she would cry.

All through this piece of the meeting, ordinarily around forty minutes, I would stay quiet. Be that as it may, over the long haul, gradually, she changed her reenactment. Indeed she did less murmuring and investigating and invested more energy shaking and murmuring.

At last, after numerous long periods of having me lie on the floor, as I began to walk to the centre of the space to rest, she grasped my hand and drove me to a recliner all things considered. She had me sit. She strolled over to the cabinet, pulled down a book, and slithered into my lap. "Tell me a story," she said.

Furthermore, as I began she said, "Rock." From there on, Sandy sat in my lap and we shook and understood books. It was anything but a fix, yet it was a decent beginning. Also, even though she needed to go through a horrendous care fight as her organic dad, her maternal grandma, and her non-permanent family battled for her care, I'm satisfied to say that at last, Sandy did well.

Her advancement was slow yet consistent, particularly after the authority case was settled for the temporary family, with whom she spent the remainder of her life as a youngster. At times, she battled, be that as it may, generally she did incredibly well. She made companions, got passing marks, and was quite kind and sustaining in her cooperation with others.

Frequently, years would go by and I wouldn't hear anything about her. In any case, much of the time, I pondered Sandy and what she had shown me in our work together. I'm satisfied to say that months prior I got an update.

She is getting along admirably. On account of the conditions of her case, I can't uncover any further subtleties. Taking everything into account, she's having the sort of fulfilling and useful life we all needed for her. Nothing could make me more joyful.

www.ingramcontent.com/pod-product-compliance
Lightning Source LLC
Chambersburg PA
CBHW031418250726
48656CB00002B/727

* 9 7 9 8 3 2 3 1 0 0 6 1 3 *